reality, distilled.
It's not the transcendent
try hold and fail,
or all wonder
well told but pale –
No.

Poetry is
reality, distilled.
It starts with the corn or the rye,
the simple things at hand,
already born, ready for the fire –
Yes.

Poetry is
reality, distilled.
It's moonshine brewing, the jar aglow,
spirits in a bottle,
tied with a rag, ready to throw –
Light it...

Poetry is
reality, distilled.
It's the alchemy of words in ferment, the fuel
in a vessel contained, the juice
for your brain, for your soul –
Ignite it!

Poetry is... (Take 2)

Ok, what is poetry again?
Here's another take –
Poetry is like maple syrup.
Poets take what is flowing out there in the world,
and boil it down to its essence.
Yeah, poetry is like maple syrup.
So whether that essence is
bitter or sweet, kind or mean, rough or easy,
a poet tells you – in a few precious drops –
what just happened out there...
or in there.
So you're sayin' that prose is the sap? Yep.
That prose goes on and on and on, and just won't stop?
Yep. The sap.
You writer of prose, can't you boil down those words?
Can't you tell me if it's
up or down, hot or mellow, high or low
without writing a g.d. book?
Here's what I'm sayin' –
Can't you tell it to me short and sweet?
Can't you make poetry for me?

Almost
Whole

Almost
Whole

Almost Whole

New and Selected Poems

New Friends, Old Friends

Mark Bohrer

"A poem...begins as a lump in the throat,
a sense of wrong, a homesickness, a lovesickness."
Robert Frost

More poetry can be found here:
www.markbohrer.us

Front cover photograph is by Maxine Raynal / Flickr
"Lever de lune en Méditerranée"
Thank you Maxine for a wonderful composition!
https://www.flickr.com/photos/108892623@N02/21695194710

Photo accompanying "Across The Knife Edge" is by Dan McGinness
from his solo winter 2014 hike of Mt. Katahdin in Maine
http://dmoutdoors.blogspot.com/2014/04/mt-katahdin-baxter-hamlin-peak-solo-in.html

Photo accompanying "The Hard Part" is by Kriszta Hajdu
https://www.pinterest.com/brainstewska/photography/

All other artwork licensed for use or public domain

Second Edition: January 2022
ISBN-13: 978-1987459135
ISBN-10: 198745913X

To Debbie
For the poetry we write together

You and me
Wading along the Little Miami shore
Holding hands
We can't release

A Good In-Land Town (2015 – 2018)

High Tide On The Other Side Of The Earth (2015 – 2016)

A Crowd Of Joy At The Door (2014 – 2015)

Small Universe (1979 – 1987)

Foreword

"Almost Whole" by Mark Bohrer is the kind of poetry that one must live with for a time. The scope and richness are so deep, and at times so deliciously intense, that the reader must pause to savor the delicate fullness of his work. It is simultaneously sophisticated and accessible.

His creative path journeys both inward and outward. Everyday connections to immediate nature such as in 'The Big Room', allow an evening walk with dogs to become an exploration of metaphysics. The reader moves from being anchored in community to expanding into the universe. Narratives of place tether the loftiness of the rise of consciousness.

His longer poems are grounded in classical tradition. He hails from the climes of Anne Bradstreet, Henry Wadsworth Longfellow, and Robert Frost. It is a location known as the Valley of the Poets. That energy permeates his words. Making his pen an 'arrow of time' he describes his connection to the warm New England homes and the ancestors who lived there

> *Careful joins of the old growth cedar*
> *trace invisibly on my skin.*
>
> *Yet I feel*
> *the minds of men*
> *who made these simple frames*

However, his range of poetry harmonizes with the extensiveness of his vision. His lyrical poetry is a delight of both sight and sound. From explorations of the contemporary to homages to past poets. His haiku are contemplative and demonstrate his opening thoughts on poetry as "reality distilled"

the black ink stands small
tries to fill the empty page
white space fills the rest

This volume takes us on a path leading our shared experiences of a school band and a hometown football gamed to an inspiring philosophical ride on an Existential roller coaster to arrive with a longing for spiritual awareness while 'Waiting In The Churchyard'.

The only thing one might disagree with in this work is the title... "Almost Whole". This is a voyage to wholeness. It is the tour in tour de force.

Bob Whelan
Rockport, Massachusetts
January 2022

Almost Whole

The sea runs tonight.
The moon is almost full.
Stand with me at the narrow straits,
where the Merrimack meets the tide.
Gaze across the bay, under the gibbous night,
watch at anchor, how the island rides.
Against the dark, it plumbs the deepening sea.
Breathe in the cool night-air, and look!
Even the wind on the water moves to the lunar pull!
Keeping her date, the moon rests on our shoulders.
Starlight gleams from a distant shore.
Moon-blanched rocks stand above the flood,
the Joppa Flats are gone. Salt-marsh birds rest in the reeds.
Tonight they hide, choosing to let the tide work its force.
Keeping her promise, on her ephemeris, the moon moves,
the waters rise, and our river changes course,
bearing in the salt, a salve for the wounded.
Tonight we receive the tide's ephemeral and ageless balm.

In this long arrival of life, I am reached
by a tide that stands full at the strand.
The water lies full at my feet, cresting
where I stand, where I am, cresting the shore.
Good comes in, comes in, to me as to each,
retreats and then, calls out, have some more.
In this run, ebbs strife.
Good flows in, arriving, and arriving.
It is enough. I take, I sample, I store.

Tonight there is no retreat,
no gliding taking in the wash of the strand,
no draw of the tide, no grating roar.
Tonight the same salten sea rises within;
the same ocean river courses the inner shore.
It runs in this temple, in these freshets and veins.
Tonight it arrives, bearing the same cure.
I am not as wounded as I thought –
no knife to withdraw.
I am speechless, struck dumb to my shallow core
by the depth of the sea that surrounds.
The breath of the sea-air touches my face,
sea and stars go still; wind and water, no sound.
From afar, tide and moon in silent tune embrace.
I see no struggle, no pain, no sadness, no sorrow –
no need. The moon is almost full.

What if I am standing at the waters of Charon,
in range of his searching eye? The ferryman, ready on his raft,
ready with his constrictors, his leathers, his binds,
gliding by, on the dark river Styx, silent, his eye all hunger –
what if he found me with no want, no hunger, no need?
What if he turned downstream?
Tonight the ferryman turns his eye,
and misses one.
Ready with his constrictors, he turns from me,
and I unwind what was taut.
The cord of discord is loosed, prevented, undone.
I have finally gone to school. I have finally learned
how to be untaught.
What I have is enough.
The night-air is sweet. The tide is full.
The darkling plain but reveals
the glimmering light of the stars.

October 2016   North Andover, Mass.

Postscript to "Almost Whole" – My Poetic Response to Dover Beach

One of my favorite poems is "Dover Beach" by Matthew Arnold.

I hesitate to say this because it's such a downbeat poem. My God, I swear, if Mr. Arnold had a pistol nearby when he completed it, it might have been all over for him. As I write these words, in the latter days of an endless and endlessly downbeat election season, I can relate more than ever to the downbeat view of the human condition and human fate that's found in Dover Beach. Darkling plain indeed.

Matthew Arnold's poem is short, less than 40 lines, and very accessible. And yet it has so many layers and echoes for such a short poem. There's a good chance you read it in high school. It's been called "the most anthologized poem in the English language."

I've been carrying this poem around in my head for a while now. The thing is, as beautiful as it is, and as evocative as it is, I couldn't disagree with it more. So in addition to the words of this poem, I carried THAT thought in my head for quite a while. Somehow, Mr. Arnold got it fundamentally - if beautifully - wrong.

Well, as I carried this thought around, something happened, as things do. The mulling turned into a poem – actually starting out in response to a biography of Emily Dickinson! I was reading Jerome Charyn's "A Loaded Gun", and my response to that somehow became a response to Dover Beach. I still remember where I was in the Andover Public Library when I immediately stopped to put the words down on paper. This poem was the result.

October 2016
North Andover, Mass.

Pieces Of The Year

(2020 – 2021)

When You Knelt and Kissed The Stage At Madison Square Garden

Today is your first headline show
We are in this hall
Hallowed by music
Music that raised the rafters above
We still hear the echo

I bow before no one
Though I worship the ground
On which you walk

I tell myself again
I will not bow
Before you

You and twins and band bound onto the stage
To cheers, applause, the roar
I am with the multitude
Then you stop
You kneel facing us
You kneel to the stage
You kiss the stage

I know what you're doing
I know what this is
You bow before the holy
You hear the echoes of the voices
Hallowing this place
You kiss the stage

Now I wish to bow
I bow
Only before the god
That you bow before

Who is your god?
Who is your muse?
We seek the same god
We seek the same muse
In the hall tonight
You kiss the stage
You join the multitude
Let us pray

Thank you Brandi Carlile and band for that night
Yes, she did this
Madison Square Garden, New York City September 14, 2019
Written September 2020 North Andover, Mass.

The real thing we call God

The real thing we call God keeps reappearing
reappearing every time we give up
reappearing every time we say
God help me, I can't go on

Every time we are worn out by the friction
of other people
saying no purpose, no purpose
worn out by the friction of ourselves
worn out by the friction of life
saying no purpose, no purpose

Wait in the field of dust
in the field of dust, wait
let the rain fall
let it clear the dust
let it clear the field
let the water run
let the river run
let it carry you to the quiet
let the silt find its place
let the water find its home
let the water clear
let the water still
wait wait

When we stand or sit
empty empty of this life
when we carry nothing
but this heavy emptiness
when we carry nothing
the real thing appears
God God
thank you

How can God appear out of nothing?
wait wait

December 2019 North Andover, Mass.

No Ordinary Time

It's an ordinary day
Unlike any other
I feel like I'm falling
Falling and wondering
How far can I fall
While I stand still at the counter?
I hold tight to my cup
Of coffee and soymilk
It's an ordinary day
As I take a sip
I watch the news
But I don't drop the cup
But maybe I should

Something holds the cup
Something holds me up
I am held by a hand
A hand I can't name
I cannot name what holds me
But I see what it does
On this ordinary day
I drink my coffee
I take a breath

I think of you
All of you are here
All of you are around me
All of you hold me up
May I do this for you
On this ordinary day
Unlike any other
You hold me up
May I do this for you
On this ordinary day
You are here

March 2020 North Andover, Mass.

We Are All Falling

This I found
The best poems start
With a feeling of falling
Whether I write or read
The same is true
The bottom drops out
And I go through
Hopefully, the poem catches the fall
I find that falling is a good place to start

But what if you're already falling?
Before the poem starts
What then?
I'm falling all the time now
We fall
From one minute to the next
So used to it, the fall feels like life
Every minute, we are all falling into the future

Whether I sit or stand
The same is true
The bottom drops out
And I go through
If the poem catches the fall
Then falling is a good place to start

June 2020   North Andover, Mass.

I.N.D.Y. 2020

I'm Not Dead Yet, aye, aye, not yet –
And yet – is what I say an act of defiance or just talking?
Yet – It is enough, 'twill serve, aye, and Gomorrah
Yet – Though we are innocent, or not, we face it the same
Yet – Though the New Year has come, the year in review is not done
Yet – We are not done, though many are, aye, many are
Yet – For so many, so many gone too soon, it doesn't mean we forget
Yet – To know brings resolve, and THAT we carry, alone AND together
Yet – Together is the strongest of all, unbreakable vow
Yet – A new year begins, knowing we're not ready, not knowing the course
Yet – I am not ready to give up
Yet – I am not dead – not yet – not yet – *I said – not yet –*
I must ask this – I ask this –
Yet – Are you with us? Are you with us?
Aye
Aye

January 1st, 2021 North Andover, Mass.

35 mm Color Slide Film, Only

We look through a glass, clearly
In color this time, brightly
A picture in hand, simply
It shows what we had, sadly
We sit in a room, darkly
The past on a screen, truly
Light opens our eyes, lovely

March 2021 North Andover, Mass.

13

Shell Found On The Ohio Shore

You and me
Wading along the Little Miami shore
A balancing act
Sometimes hand in hand
Testing rocks in the shallows
In and out of the quiet water
An early Saturday, a misty morn
Exploring this river strand

You and me
On this misty morn
Down the muddy hillside
Down from river road
Down from the old farmhouse
The oldest one around
1790 weathered on the sign

What we want today is older
Older than George, older than Adam
A million years of folding, more
Time turning, time from way over yonder
We're looking through the layers
Seeking footprints of life
Walking on an ancient sea floor
Swimming in ancient oceans
Now old rocks, to gather in a can

Ohio used to be ocean front, an ocean busy with life
Lives with their own purpose, sapiens not in sight
Busy burying time capsules for us to find
Hidden messages in the sand, turned into stones

Already one slip, for me a wet shoe
A cold good morning hello, but a worthy fossil found
The can filling with rocks and mud
On a cold misty morn, balancing on these rocks
Hand in hand along the Little Miami shore

A surprise, surprise –
At our feet, we spy – the shell – and a toad! –
The toad jumps away, we reach together –
Two hands get the prize –
Hands together, we hold a spiral shell –
What are we holding?

We turn our palms, side by side
Sand and grit, and how, an ocean shell?
Fresh from the ocean, the ocean is here?
It's true, this shell is new
No fossil, you, our saltwater friend
We look at each other, we look back
We stand in silt and muck, baffled
We gaze at your spiral unfolding

Were you thrown from some truck by the hand of a child?
Did you fall from a pocket, from a mystery locket?
How did this message land on this inner shore?
On a mystery tour, how did you travel the miles?

Around our feet, your early cousins rest
Resting in sand turned to stone
Impressions on the soft sea floor
Revealed by this river
But for all our puzzling
We can't reveal what we hold
But for all our puzzling
We can't release our hands
From your spiral unfolding
We can't release our hands
We touch the ocean inside
An ocean we found today
You and me
Wading along the Little Miami shore
Holding hands
We can't release

May 2020 North Andover, Mass.

We are all different, we are all the same
(A Poem for Rose and Kayla)

The sun shines, the skies clear
This warm and bright new day
Silently proclaims
Our hands touch, our faces near
This sunny moment stays
So quiet, we speak the same

Our eyes speak, we both say
You are the one I choose
With you I lose my fear
Our eyes speak, we both say
Will you share my name?

Look into my eyes
Let me tell you who I am
Love is true, love is wise
Inside my name
I find yours
Hidden within
Like an anagram

The sun shines, our eyes see
A world of acceptance
A world to ease the pain
I step into a world of love
When you call my name

We are all different
We are all the same
We are all different
We are all the same

Always remember
There is nothing else worth sharing
Like the love that let us share our name

PS with thanks to the Avett Brothers for the closing lines
July 2021 North Andover, Mass.

Unequal or Equal

Do you mind
if I tip
the scales, press
a thumb, place
a weight on the
balance of
my side?
It will tip
my way –
Is that ok?
Do you mind?

Do you mind
if I start
the race halfway
to the prize?
Why, we still have the same chance –
We start the same.
We stand
side by side.
Ready? You have two laps to go.
if I have
but one –
Do you mind?

Do you mind
if my house is on
this side
of the tracks?
I really don't do
well with smoke.
Do you mind?

If things are
"equaled up" –
do I have to give you
what's already mine?
Is that
what you say?
If you get
won't you take
this and that
from me and mine?
If you get
won't I have to give?
Would that
be fair?
If we don't –
Do you mind?

Oh, and by the way
if someone asks about
this unequal-equal thing –
I never said this.
We never spoke.
Do you mind?

January 2, 2022 North Andover, Mass.
In memory of the poet Blaine Hebbel
With thanks
Nobody did what you did
Occupy everything

Variations On A Christmas Day

Walking in the ice and rain – out early Christmas day –
From my phone – into the silent air – notes of the Kanon play.
A Variation starts – the piano alone – but I hear broken notes.
Taken from the song I know – into the stillness – they float.
Alone they echo – like broken pieces of the year –
A variation on the theme – that's what I hear.
A variation on the year – that's what I feel.

Walking on the snow and ice of a Christmas morn,
The piano sounds, the old tune takes shape, as if reborn.
The notes of the Kanon find each other, they join, they weave.
The artist helps us, the tune takes air, a voice, the music speaks.
Carried over the frosted land,
The music holds me up, it takes my hand.
The music reminds me, the season of good is always here.
I never know what I need until it appears.

In this season of dark – in this season of light –
May you find one another – may your heart stay bright –
May what you need appear –
May find a Merry Christmas and may it be –
A Happy New Year!

PS With thanks to pianist George Winston
and his "Variations on the Kanon by Johann Pachelbel"
December 25, 2021 North Andover, Mass.

The Big Room

(2016 – 2019)

<u>Introduction to "The Six Grandfathers" – Where This Poem Started</u>

Several years ago, I wrote a poem titled "Ozymandias In Reverse". The poem told of a person traveling in the desert who came upon great carved stones lying about on the land, and a tower built of these stones. The person wondered how these great building stones and tower came to be. The poem was an attempt to take the idea of Percy Bysshe Shelley's "Ozymandias" and turn it on its head. It wondered if a great structure, rather than falling into wreck and decay with the passage of time, could somehow come into being, could come to greatness with the passage of time.

The narrator of "Ozymandias in Reverse" comes to realize that the reason the great stones and tower are there may not be due the power of the hand that shaped and built them – they may only be there because everything else around them had worn away. The stones that remained had withstood the test of time.

Then I saw a beautiful picture of Mount Rushmore, a picture taken from the air, showing Washington's face in profile. His face was like the prow of a ship, gazing out onto America. I had visited Mount Rushmore many decades before and had an image of the monument in my mind, but this picture struck me differently. Instead of us looking at the figures on Mount Rushmore and wondering about them, what do those figures think when they look out at this land?

Then another question came to mind – what about the figures that are missing from this monument? What about those who lived on this land for millennia before the Europeans arrived? These great figures from our past – whether they are present in granite or in spirit – what do they see when they look out at their country, when they look at us? That's where I started.

North Andover, Mass.

The Six Grandfathers

Under the sky, bright with the crown of sunrise, the land sits dark, waiting.
Alone, the night still around me, I stand in the Dakota park, watching.
At first light, I see a land and sky newly made, washed clean
    by the night's hard rain.
From afar, four colossi gaze, their dawn mountain serene
    above the plains.
Hidden from my eyes, guarding the native land and sky, two other faces reside.
On the mountain, with the four, the Warrior and the Healer-who-sees
    still preside.

The faces of the four, my eyes do plain receive.
On the inner eye, the two of the spirit fall.
I gaze at them, all these times, alone in this common hall,
yet to my mind, do their words and deeds conceive?
Here is what I lack, pray tell me how? How to know these six?
They answer me quick, an easy fix. Turn around the scene.

[compass North]

The eyes of Washington keep watch from the mountaintop,
    as if our soul to measure.
A gift from the sculptor, an offering from his workshop,
    the visage whole, he sees.
The ancient humors show themselves, in proper measure handsome –
the sanguine, the melancholic –
the ready hope and slow anger, leavened by patient earn'ed wisdom.
How to see what he sees?
Turn around the scene.
I follow his gaze, as he surveys the far countryside of time.
I follow his eyes, wonder at their demand,
do the people and this land
still earn the temper of this man?

[compass East]

Jefferson's eyes look east to the sun, as if ever to the new day open.
With authoring words he wrote, not with his own, but the creator's pen.
His words still ring true through the world, self-evident,
for all who would gather in the light of the new day.
But his life left many in chains, left a bell still ringing in the American night,
a bell of warning, of time lost, of pain,
of old scars from the lash, of shackles that remain.

My eyes travel with his, with history our guide.
On our own corps of discovery from above,
I fly with the author across the great divide.
On my return, I see anew the same land he loved.
Our history near, I hear his words echo in me.
Standing here, I am left wiser but less happy.

[compass South]

Lincoln guided a nation through the wilderness of war,
our Abraham.
I follow his eyes to the south, to freedom and justice for all, to a new country.
The United States.
He told us why we fought, and what was right.
Although his sepulcher journey passed into the night,
we have the hope of this man, his still living words, eloquent.
His eyes look to us
to complete, to dedicate, to consecrate, to hallow
what his words inaugurated.
His eyes look past me, still brooding over this land.

[compass West]

T.R. defends the land. He looks west, great vistas in sight –
There he fought the good fight.
His big stick diplomacy had its day,
but here is what stayed:
He opposed the narrow few, spoke for the common man –
and a gift that was new –
He bound us to a vision of the common land,
to protect our true nature
from our own careless hand.

[compass to the Land, compass to the Sky]

For those of us who came before, may the journey be told –
For those of us who hunted on plains and woods to the east –
For those of us who lived here a thousand summers, ten-fold –
For those of us who crossed the western bridge,
        before it returned to the seas –
two faces are hidden in this land, in this sky, never old.

Black Elk and Crazy Horse, we know their names;
their spirit winters in these hills and pines.
Do they long to tell us of tribes, our kin, alive, not past?
Do they long to tell us our story, our country, recast?
I stand in darkness at sunrise, I stand here, held fast.
Do they see one land, one history, one people, at last?

[The Six Grandfathers]

I stand on their mountain, I look from their summit.
I gaze to the compass points of spirit and granite.
To the north and south, to the east and west, to the earth and sky –
How to know these six?
At today's first light, the six grandfathers reply –
Turn around the scene.

Their eyes measure and judge,
in hope, in righteous anger, in compassion and justice, in sorrow and healing,
showing what was earned, what was borrowed, what was taken,
and what has been given.

Our grandfathers guide us, there are four in books.
On this mountain, I see more than four; more directions are fixed.
For our people, in our story today, on the mountain here, there are six.
From where I stand, I follow their gaze, they show me where to look.

January 2018   North Andover, Mass.

A View of the Black Hills From Black Elk Peak, South Dakota

"The Six Grandfathers" is the Lakota Sioux name for the mountain known today as Mount Rushmore. As "The Six Grandfathers", the mountain was part of the route that Lakota leader Black Elk took in a spiritual journey that culminated at Black Elk Peak. Following a series of military campaigns from 1876 to 1878, the United States asserted control over the area, a claim that is still disputed on the basis of the 1868 Treaty of Fort Laramie. Among American settlers, the peak was known variously as Cougar Mountain, Sugarloaf Mountain, Slaughterhouse Mountain, and Keystone Cliffs. It was named Mount Rushmore in 1885 during a prospecting expedition by Charles Rushmore, David Swanzey (husband of Carrie Ingalls), and Bill Challis. (from Wikipedia)

Gerard Baker, a Native American, was appointed superintendent of Mount Rushmore by the National Park Service in 2004. He was the first Native American to serve in that role at Mount Rushmore. He worked to bring the Indian perspective to the interpretive program at the National Memorial. The account at this link was researched as part of the Ken Burns special on the National Parks: https://tinyurl.com/gerard-baker

The Big Room
Or an evening walk in the rhyming universe

The evening sky brightens outside, and draws light from my room.
The dogs, impatient at my feet, want to move, let's leave this tomb.
I laugh, is the workday through? Their leashes on, and mine, undone,
we step into the outer room, now the realm of the setting sun.

It's eventide, half-summer, as we step into the gloaming,
into that room with no ceiling, the three of us go roaming.
Into the warm quiet nightfall, we enter this swirling place.
Leaving our home, my dogs take me on a trip through time and space.

The fading light is stealing, background radiation, fleeing,
new stars and planets are appearing, pearls in a pink champagne sea.
As the swirling sky darkens, what's left still ignites my brain.
It leaves me with this feeling, our familiar world is strange.

It looks as if I'm standing on the edge of an open field.
It looks like a man with two dogs – instead the infinite, revealed.
I feel the arrow of time, the sky aquiver with twilight
My hand draws the bow of the Archer, his dart flies across the night.

In this room, my hand can reach to the edge of space and beyond.
From me to that star, I could skip a stone across this pond.
Can my spirit bear the lightness of The All within my reach?
Yet here I am, in the big room, dizzy, with dogs at my feet.

Overhead, there to the right, shines Vega, Mister Sagan's star.
He had a billion or two to share, but this one was the door.
Twenty-five light years, a short step away, Contact was the book,
where Ms. Foster met her Dad, or an alien with a kindly look.

How can all this be so welcoming? It could squash me like a bug.
But it doesn't seem so inclined – somehow it feels more like a hug.
A hadron glow still warms the sky, and the worlds around each star.
The radiation might be dangerous, but still, it warms my heart.

Summer solstice, June 2017, North Andover, Mass.
This poem was selected as a finalist in the 2019 Robert Frost Foundation Poetry Contest.

The main stars of the constellation Sagittarius the Archer
also make the familiar shape of the teapot.
The center of the Milky Way galaxy is in Sagittarius.

Introduction to "My First Home"

Four days before the Spring Concert, I got a text from Justin Smalley, Director of the North Andover HS Band:

> Justin: "Last year I read a poem for the seniors titled Last Days. Was wondering if you had anything original that you have written that would be appropriate for the last days in the band room?"
> Mark: "No, I don't. I could find something. Or I'll write it. :-)"
> Justin: "I like your last option, if you have time."

Ok, write it. So I went to work. I decided it had to be ready for the spring concert. Justin said I could have one page in the program. I had 4 days.

To get things rolling, I sent out a request to close friends, other parents with kids in band, for ideas, memories, memes. Boy, did that help. I had my own, since my two kids went through the wonderful music program we have in North Andover. After many years supporting my kids in the North Andover Middle School and High School music programs, you have a lot of memories. Many ideas came in from parents. I tried to distill it down. The theme came from what I had heard over and over again from the kids. This poem is what came out.

Go Scarlet Knight Marching Band!

PS One of the best things about the Spring concert was that my son Nick read this poem from the North Andover HS auditorium stage at the concert that night.

May 2019   North Andover, Mass.
First published on "North Andover Poets Corner" Facebook group as
the Word from the Corner, June 1, 2019

My First Home

Dut-dut-dut-dut, I feel the beat, I hear the voice. How do I explain?
We're the ones who put on a show – making music is our choice, it's our DNA –
Dut-dut-dut-dut, I feel the beat, I hear the voice. How do I explain?
We're the ones who start a show – while lying in the dirt –
lying there on a cold wet field in a white compression shirt!

I started that first day, a little scared, when I entered that holy room.
Mr. N and Mr. I prepared us – Mr. "e" was friendly – why did I feel such doom?
I knew I could make sounds, but would I make music or just a sonic boom?
What would it be like to perform together, in this symphonic playroom?

Mr. Smalley started with "Be Inspiring"; something happened as the magic spun.
We had our roles in Brass and Reeds, in Woodwinds, Percussion and Drums.
We had our roles in Color Guard and as drum majors; we made music, we made fun.
We became more than a bunch of kids, we became a family, we joined as one.

Black socks. Cream Crew. Mr. Smalley remembers my name!
An American in Africa, Primary Colors, We The People, Checkmate!
Hey band! Hey what? Let's sing "Hey Baby" in the pouring rain!
Bright lights. Chess pieces. The national anthem on the bus. A 93.8! That's 93 point 8!

We played concerts, Pep Band and Jazz Nights. We marched in town parades.
At Williamsburg and the LA Festival of Gold, we worked to make the grade.
We played for the school. We played for the town. We played for all America.
Wow, that encore performance in Nashville! Get ready, next year, it's Antarctica!

Off that backstage corridor, I became one of many, one of the chosen few.
In a plain room, my home away from home, something here was new.
In the band room, we made harmony and rhyme.
Making art, making music, we also made family time.
At home you find your family – something happened as we rehearsed –
The band room is not my second home, I tell you, it's my first.

May 2019 North Andover, Mass.
North Andover is the home of the Scarlet Knight Marching Band

The Fifth Hexagram: Waiting Is

Enter the soft word.
The best is assumed today.
The mouth opens with hope.
The mouth does not speak.
The eyes open today.
The eyes open even in the smoke and dust.
The eyes open but do not speak.
Do not want.
Do not have.
Emptiness is.
Opportunity is.
The 5th Hexagram is.
Open then not is.
Open then not is.
Whole at the bottom is.
The empty waters over heaven is.
Opportunity is.
Waiting is.
Assume best intent without moving.
Use your soft word today.
The eyes open today.
The Fifth Hexagram is.
Waiting is.

September 2019 North Andover, Mass.

36

<u>my haiku about haiku</u>

1
here are some haiku
standing here looking at you
say kon'nichiwa

2
the words are loaded
in the poetic pistol they wait
bang! flowers appear!

3
simple only, so
around, it sees, it hears, so
in the moment, so

4
the haiku – not clear
a few words say what they say
everyone says what?

俳句についての私の俳句

俳句

the black ink stands small
tries to fill the empty page
white space fills the rest

De-versification

or news of my divestment from The Vintage Book Of Contemporary American Poetry

I watch your angels
dance on the head of a pin.
I wait for music.

When I play your verse,
angels dance; my heart stands still.
The shoe never drops.

Selections From The Western Canon in Haiku

俳句の西部教会

All those books to read
Skip the Latin, skip the Greek
Here is what you need!

Knowledge, truth, beauty!
Here's the Canon in haiku!
Wisdom! Brevity!

Homer's Odyssey
Odysseus sails
Ten years pass, mom has suitors!
He's back! Tragedy!

The Old Testament
In the beginning
God gave his people a land
Messiah? Still waiting...

The New Testamant
Jesus was made man
He walked on water, died, rose
Paul made the franchise

The Works of William Shakespeare
Will wrote sonnets, plays –
comedies and tragedies –
get over it – Will wrote them!

Walt Whitman
He wrote "Leaves of Grass"
He's America's poet
We don't read poetry

Emily Dickinson
More than nobody
She would not stop for death
But I stop for her

Anna Karenina by Tolstoy
Sad anna, sad wife
Run away with your Vronsky
A train? Now we're sad!
    (spoiler alert: yes she throws herself in front of a train!)

Sigmund Freud and Psychoanalysis
Oedipus complex?
Id? Ego? Super-ego?
It's just a cigar!

Jean-Paul Sartre and Existentialism
Condemned to freedom!
To be alive, we must choose!
I still don't get it

The Lord of the Rings by J.R.R. Tolkien
Frodo has the ring
Sauron searches with his eye
Three movies to rule them all!
    (No six! Eight? Eleventeen?)

And one more – this is by my daughter Jillian
(caution - spoiler alert!)

Harry Potter and the Half Blood Prince (book 6)
by J.K. Rowling
Pensieve shows the past
Horcruxes must be destroyed
Snape kills Dumbledore!

Thus Ends the Western Canon for Today
The lesson is done
You may not know it all
But at least you know some

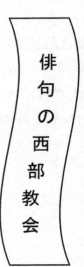

俳句の西部教会

The Football Poems #1

Poetry before a football game? Well, of course!
I had the chance on Friday to introduce the North Andover HS and Westford
Academy teams with a poem. Thank you to Sara Durkin for being open to the
idea of a football poem before the game. The Scarlet and Black chorus were
lined up to sing the national anthem - and she gave me the mic.

Before The Kickoff
Two teams will take the field - Scarlet Knights, meet the Grey Ghosts.
To the captains - are your teams ready to give their most?
First honor sportsmanship, first honor fair play.
Then seek to be champion, then seize the day.
Both teams come here to compete,
both teams come here to win.
One will leave the field with the banner,
may all leave the field
as friends.

Here is the video on YouTube:
https://tinyurl.com/football-poem
Posted to the North Andover Poets Corner on Facebook, October 28, 2018

The idea for this little poem all happened last week. On Tuesday night, Gayle Heney, a past Poet Laureate of North Andover, handed me the email address of Ray Ahern, a cameraman for NA Cable Access. NACAM records and broadcasts the HS football games, and Ray thought it would be cool to have a poem at the coin toss. So I wrote these lines over the next few days.

I arrive early to find Ray (who I had never met) before the game. As I talked to him, it was now clear that this was his idea only, nobody else there was on board. Like the PA announcer or Athletic Director or anybody. But he did have a good idea. And I had my little football poem. So now what?

I needed Sara Durkin, NAHS Chorus Director. I knew that reading it before the national anthem would be perfect. Would Sara be ok with it? Since I'm on the board of the North Andover Music Association, the music booster group, she knew who I was. So I headed to the HS auditorium, and found her with the chorus where they had just finished rehearsing. I explained what I wanted to do...she was a little confused until I said I was North Andover's Poet Laureate. Then it all made sense to her! She gave an enthusiastic yes. Thank you Sara. Should I do one for this Friday's next playoff game? (PS I did!)

The Football Poems #2

Are You Ready?
The players are ready. Two great teams are here.
Hey town – yo Freddys and Bettys – are YOU ready?
Hey town – give 'em a cheer! (Say YEAH!)
Time for talkin' is done allright,
Both teams done waiting, ready to have fun tonight!
The chorus is ready to sing for the town.
The band and the cheerleaders are ready to get up and get down!
May you play with a love of life, ready for fame!
May you play with a love of the game!
ARE YOU READY? (Say YEAH!)

The Football Poems #3

On Friday night, the North Andover HS football team continued their playoff run - and I was there with a poem to start the night! This was the third round of the playoffs, and my third "football poem". Here it is. Like the previous two times, Sara Milaschewski Durkin was open to the idea, and gave me the chance to perform this for the crowd, right before the NAHS Scarlet and Black chorus sang the national anthem.

A cool fall night, a high school sporting rite,
a friendly fight, under Friday night lights!
The Warriors of Lincoln-Sudbury
face the North Andover Scarlet Knights!
Who will taste the victory cup? Who will reach the heights?
Take your shot, give it all you've got,
but remember first what you've been taught:
Respect is 1 2 and 3 – self, opponent, the game -
May these your principles be.
When all is said, when all is done,
When you meet to shake hands, no matter who has won,
Let's have this to say: That was a great game, that was fun!

PS Fortunately the rain held off until after the national anthem. Then it rained. Then the rain became a downpour. Buckets. North Andover played great, really impressive, ending up with a dominating 42-0 win. Wow is right. I lasted until halftime when we had a 28-0 lead. In spite of the rain, North Andover did have fun!

Posted to the North Andover Poets Corner on Facebook, November 10, 2018

The Football Poems #4

Here's a football poem for the championship game tomorrow! North Andover Scarlet Knights Football team will be playing the King Philip Warriors in Gillette Stadium Friday evening at 7:30PM. The Division 2 Superbowl! I probably won't get the same chance to read it like I did at NAHS Walsh Stadium, so here is my 4th poem in this vein. Good luck to all, and especially go Scarlet Knights!

Catch It!

Wow, what a place! Take a look around!
We're in the Patriot's castle! Hey, is that Brady's crown?
King Philip Warriors – meet the North Andover Scarlet Knights.
Green & Gold and Scarlet & Black – two teams are ready to reach the heights!
Go ahead, enjoy the sights, enjoy the day,
But while the ball is in the air, don't get carried away.
You got this, you know this game,
We may be in the Patriot's castle, but the field's the same.
The field's the same.
Just play the way you trained, you will own the bracket.
While the ball is in the air, have some fun – catch it!

PS So did North Andover win the state championship? They did - but it was tough. They won 6-0 on a lone 2nd quarter touchdown (missed point after). But they held tough against a strong physical team in King Philip Regional. An undefeated season. A Division 2 state football championship. What a run.

Posted to the North Andover Poets Corner on Facebook, November 29, 2018

Shards of Dylan
(directions: read as fast as you can)

I feel the steel, it cuts me deep.
Still I reach for it, it's real, it keeps
the hand I want so very much
away. I cannot feel or touch.
Luck looks up, says take a leap.
But where I live, I stay there.
In my church, I say a prayer.
What will I do tomorrow?

I turn to you, inside I burn.
Tell me what I have to earn.
I hope this doesn't take me down.
This is where I live, it's my town.
Tears and fears on the sinner's face,
an empty room, a womb for grace.
No escape, a door I cannot trace,
I see a frame, an open pane.
A window there, yet I remain.
I stare into the open air.
If I go, I know not where.
For still I face tomorrow.

July 2017 North Andover, Mass.

47

The Hard Part

Lyrics from the song, music by Joe Bohrer III

A cold winter day, I'm walking the road.
Got a ride this far, now on my own.
Crossing these fields, hard empty rows,
Crossing this town, this was my home.
Nothing but scrabble, winter stubble and hay,
Nothing is here, it's all cut away.
Still I smile, still I smile,
Is this what's left for you and me?

I look back there, over my shoulder,
Is that my life or is it a fable?
So much has passed, so much has passed.
I left the hard part for last.

How can I feel so down? How can I feel so low?
Where are you? What do I owe?
This world is nothing but ice and gravel.
I left the long road for the end of my travels.
I left the hard part for last.

I hope that you show, you said that you would.
I'm willing to wait, wait here for good.
I'm willing to wait through the hard part.
I'm willing to wait through the hard part.
Waiting here is the hard part.
Waiting here is the hard part.

My shoes are old, hah, my feet are cold,
But the sky held off, and the wind has stopped,
That thin winter sun, it helps me some.
It brings me a smile, at the end of this mile,
Standing here, at the end of this year,
Here I am, waiting for you.
Here I am, waiting for love.

Waiting here is the hard part.
Waiting here is the hard part.
I left the hard part for last.

May 2019   North Andover, Mass.

Bird Songs Of The 21st Century
(directions: read fast)

In the night
I hear the bird songs of the 21st century
Sirens in the distance – I hear them
I hear them racing somewhere
Somewhere sirens and flashing
Flashing blue lights race
Race across my sight – blue lights flashing
Flashing in my eyes – warning
Warning of something – somewhere in the night
In the night – blue lights cross
Cross my sight – and are gone
I don't see them anymore
I don't see them – they are everywhere
I don't see them – they race
They race across my sight and are gone
They have become ubiq-ubiq-
ubiquitous – I don't have – I don't have the words
I don't hear – I don't hear the sirens – they are everywhere
Sirens are the bird songs of the 21st century
Where are the birds?

November 2018 at night North Andover, Mass.

Tell why

But I write it because it's beautiful
But I write it because it hurts
But I write it because it hurts less when I do
But I write it because it's the only way out
But I write it because it's the only way in
But I write it because it's the only way to know what I know
But I write it because
 it's beautiful

June 2019 North Andover, Mass

Connected

Every pore
every cell
every breath
every heartbeat
connects me to all that is.
When I spin
is it I who turn
or is the entire world turning
around my stillness?
I am here with all my kin
only separated by this thin veil of time
only separated by this thin veil.
You touch the whole world
the whole world touches you.
You are inseparable.
You are one.
Go forth and act
knowing the power you have
connected.

June 2017 Stevens Pond, North Andover, Mass.

Learned As A Deacon:

Bending in service to another,
we find our true shape.

A Good In-Land Town

(2015 – 2018)

Poems About A Town

For those who were here before,
for those around now,
and for those who will be here later.

The title of the poem "A Good In-Land Town"
is borrowed affectionately from
A GOOD IN-LAND TOWN:
BUILDINGS & LANDSCAPES IN NORTH ANDOVER, MA
FROM 1640 – 1940
by Stephen J. Roper, with photographs by Gayton Osgood
Published by the North Andover Historical Society

A Good In-Land Town

*In August 1702, Judge Samuel Sewall wrote about his travels
to Andover – what is current day North Andover – in his diary:
"...rid with Mr. Woodhouse and Smith to Andover,
a good In-land Town, and of a good Prospect."*

A good in-land town,
she shares her name with her British twin.
But no ruler here wears the crown,
for we are home of the citizen king.
Her citizens, now or years ago,
famous or not yet so,
share in her renown.

From strands of bell, bronze and maker,
from mother, muse and meter,
from wool and woven time,
from service made sublime,
from these we make our rhyme.

A.B. the poet, you know her name,
walked to the meetinghouse,
that first simple frame.
With words, her soul did search,
and thus made poetry her church.
Simon, the well-known man,
the Mass Bay governor, was her spouse.
Yet today, the greater fame, Anne commands.

In 1806, Revere and Son poured the bell.
Lifted high in the fourth steeple by Captains Johnson and Stevens,
in the new fifth meetinghouse soon it would dwell.
When the church was the town, it called from its tower.
These tones still carry over tree, town and common,
but for all people now, it keeps the same hours.

The 19th century mills were cut – whole cloth –
    from New England's ingenious habit and spirit.
But it was the men of North Andover who made the Stevens mills,
    with Davis and Furber as the ratchet and sprocket.
In this yarn about wool,
    from the corner of Water and High Streets,
D & F sent machines to weave their twill
    to every state, and to the world.
In the rhythm and thrum of the mills,
    these men were the heartbeat.

To America and to the world,
women and men from this town went forth to serve.
Women and men heard freedom's word.
They saw a common foe and risked their lives to fight it.
They saw a wrong and tried to right it.
And those who paid with limb or life,
their families and townspeople still observe.
What these men and women gave, may we honor it.

In a good in-land town,
history is not done,
time offers more renown.
No final bell has rung,
her story is still young.

Those who serve the town,
in public place or private space,
serve it well if one must tell,
when History and common good are the guide.
Then we may go on to say
that in a good in-land town
and in America today,
the voice of the citizen has not died.

June 2018   North Andover, Mass.
This poem was read to the North Andover Selectmen at their meeting on June 18, 2018

Echoes On The Ipswich And Essex Road

This poem was read
at the Parson Barnard House
300th Birthday Celebration
September 5, 2015

Standing here,
under the sun of an early day,
warm clapboard siding
runs under my hand.
Standing here,
along the front of the old colonial,
square cut nail heads
hidden in the wood
press against my fingertips.
The strike on nail by hand-forged hammer
still echoes to my touch.
Careful joins of the old growth cedar
trace invisibly on my skin.
These old growth trees still stand,
though turned sideways on this house front,
now three hundred years.
A surprising fate, yet they remain.
Careful joins of odd length clapboard –
why these runs of five, five, four, two, four?
Careful hands chose the best lengths,
set them right
on that early day,
now three hundred years.

Half hidden behind the house, a barn stands
unmoved on its foundation of glacial stones,
stones cleared by horse and hand from this field.
A narrow diamond window stares me in the eye,
looks back into darkness.

A round-columned side porch, open like a greeting,
steps to a kitchen garden. There the mistress
once walked to raised beds,
her thyme and sage to gather.
A triangle topped pediment, half columned,
their homage to the spirit
of another past and place,
ordains the entry door. Above, bullet pane glass
paints sunlight on the stair and empty parlor floor.

Standing echoes
of first and second period men and women
are in these frames and walls.
Here, one second before,
their children, sturdy and quiet,
stood and watched from this same sunlit door.

Standing echoes of the past,
standing echoes of their minds and hands
press on me, push into my mind,
speak to me with wordless voice.
How can wood and glass and stone
ache to tell me who was here
on that early day,
now three hundred years?

They started here with rough unpainted frame
when life was rocky and hard,
and madness against neighbor
was one time too near.
A diamond window's dark light
revealed flinty souls.
On to painted saltbox, add a columned federal porch,
the frame remade
by these men and women of rising freedom,
and a rare matching rise of grace.

The men who built these frames –
The women who made these gardens –
I can feel their hands
in what they made and left.
I love their shape,
I love their rough grace
and high simplicity.

These wooden frames remain,
like markers on the shore
of an inland New England harbor,
unsurprised when seas retreated,
unmoved by passing tides.

Standing on the Ipswich and Essex road,
against my fingertips
press board and nail and hidden joins.
How can I hope to know
the minds and hands of those who crafted
these simple protections from the wind and rain?

Yet I feel
the minds of men and women
who made these simple frames.
Yet they remain,
these places to stand and sit,
to dine and play,
to divine and pray.
Echoes of men and women
are standing here,
under the sun of an early day,
now three hundred years.

May 2015   North Andover, Mass.

The 5th of July – Introduction

I walked around Ridgewood Cemetery on Salem Road yesterday. I went with the 4th of July in mind, walking and looking at the American flags. It made me think about those who served our country. Patriotism is not a simple thing. Those who serve when called by our country in time of need do so whether they support or even fully understand the purpose of the call. They serve. For those who died in the Civil War, just reading their names, ages and where these men died made me think about their sacrifice. Here are just a few of the names that I saw:

> William W Rea 1862 20 yrs old, Harpers Ferry
> Charles Scott 1864 31 yrs. old. Salisbury NC
> Wm. H. Hardwell 1863 24 yrs old (stone too worn to read location)
> Andrew J. Fish 1863 31 yrs old. New Orleans
> Samuel G. Phelps 1864 28 yrs old. Andersonville GA
> Charles M. Bridges 1862 31 yrs. old. Natchez Miss.

Who were the volunteers? Who were the conscripts? Some of the cemetery stones record this part of their stories, but many only list their ages and where they died in service.

Sometimes being a patriot is taking a stand that brings revile and scorn, sometimes for life. Our town's best example is William Symmes of North Andover (then Andover). He broke the stalemate on Massachusetts approving the US Constitution, against the specific direction of town meeting. A lawyer and civic leader, he left town shortly after, never to return, even for his father's funeral. Civic patriots are worthy of note as well.

Patriotism is not simple. I was left with the feeling that all we can do to honor their sacrifices is how we live, and the stands we take. That's what I thought about in this poem that I wrote a few years ago. The poem started in that same cemetery at the annual Memorial Day ceremony.

July 7, 2018 North Andover, Mass.

P.S. Here's the story of North Andover's William Symmes: https://tinyurl.com/williamsymmes

The 5th Of July

On the day I was born,
my mom stood on the battlefield.
Not a woman for dramatic entrances,
and even though her doctor warned,
she went, she didn't want to miss the tour.
She went to hear the old historian,
to stand amongst the crowd in the morning dew,
to stand in the blue and gray dawn,
feet hurting, waiting expectantly.

I listened as my mom retold,
in the voice of the woman guide,
words that carried us past the span of the living,
how we came to stand upon that field,
words that summoned the watch-fires
of a hundred circling camps.
In the mist, we felt the eyes of soldiers watching,
eyes that told of fateful lightning and swift sword.
Hearkening the sounds of battle to our ears,
I was there as the historian spoke.

No longer a field, but the place of a battle.
No longer a field, but the place of rest.
For some, all ended here.
No longer a field, but the place of victory
and defeat, paid the same, with lives and blood.
No longer a field, but now a place.

The historian spoke, as she pointed to the high ground,
"See the stones and granite markers on that crest."
Against the sky, our eyes saw stone on standing stone.
As if in marching columns, they passed from our sight.
Unspoken, unsaid, but not unseen,
known at least by some,
these stones pave the road of freedom.

No longer a field, but a place to walk
in peace, from this day forward.
No longer a field, but a place to stand,
a place to stand and see one other,
a place to know,
to know we are brother and sister to one another,
brother and sister to those who rest on this field,
brother and sister bound by those who have gone before.

They fought on the 4th.
On that day, some laid down their task.
Their work brought us here.
Do we know
we were summoned by their call?
We stand on their field.
It's the 5th of July.
They brought us this far, but could go no further.
The unfinished work is ours,
their unspoken call is heard.

Today is the 5th of July,
the day we were born.

July 2016 North Andover, Mass.

Among The Names

Standing on this cold field
Surrounded by stones and names
We get cold feet
Unsure where we stand in this world
Or the next

Among the stones and names
All we can do is listen, and stand in the quiet
Among still grasses, standing stones, fallen leaves
Among the dead
Grateful for any message
Unsure what we'd do if one came
Still we listen

Among the dead
There's an inside joke, perhaps a nod, an unseen wink
An elbow in the ribs
A stifled laugh, a quieting hand to shush the lips
A secret smile
They can no longer laugh out loud
But they get the joke
They get it
For they saw the whole show
Bought the ticket, paid full price too

Standing among the names
Their hushed unspoken message
This message that they earned
Silently is heard
Ok, it's ok
Your time, enjoy
This cold field, enjoy
Your cold feet too
Until you get the joke
Until you find your name
Among the dead
Grateful be

October 2015 Old Burial Ground, Academy Road   North Andover, Mass.

Be Still

The stones listen
to the song in the air.
Birdsong and low voices mingle,
carry their pleasant tune
soft and melodious
onto our ears.

The voices and songs
of our brothers and sisters
resting nearby today
still carry in the air,
soft and melodious.

Though they be still
their song carries soft and low in the air
still.
Be still and listen.
Be still.

September 2015 Cincinnati, Ohio

High Tide On The Other Side Of The Earth

(2015 – 2016)

High Tide On The Other Side Of The Earth

Neither Achaean, nor Spartan,
nor Trojan, nor Hellene –
other climes, other ages
are father and mother to me.
Neither Agamemnon, nor Odysseus,
nor Hector, nor Achilles –
other battles, other voyages
did scar and weather this skin.
If I am none of these, why do I remain
the soldier never home from the war,
the sailor lost on the sea?
If I am no man,
with no ship and no crew,
why am I drawn by the tide?
Why am I pulled to the deep?
Why do I still hear the siren?
Why does she sing to me?

From where I stand, as if lashed to a mast –
I hear the same call – I hear her!
Her song of terror and desire –
I hear her singing to me!
I can barely stand here – I'm torn apart –
Torn between
what I have and what I want.
I tear at my bonds, terrified and yet – be still!
I hear her singing to me!

I hear the singing from every direction,
on the tide that tears me apart;
I hear singing from within and without,
the inarticulate song of the heart.

With a clap, it's released –
in a flash, transformed –
no longer a song, it's now a weapon,
like a javelin thrown, across the deep,
across the ages, coming hard at me.
It pierces me so quickly, no time for a smile.
Impossible I hear spoken, my voice from the air.
It pierces me so quickly, the speed closes its own tear.
I'm left standing, stunned and wondering,
what just reached me here, what's new?
What can I learn from what pierces me?
What can I learn from what cuts me in two?

Is there any difference between all of you and me?
We've both been struck by the same divine energy.
But I had the great good luck to see and to know –
to watch myself cut in two,
to watch myself healed,
to know this is what I asked for,
to know this is what I feel.
I had the great good luck
to hear the call, the cry,
to feel the tide beyond the horizon,
the high tide from the other side.

Sto telos, sto telos –
neither terror, nor desire,
nor battles, nor bonds
have their say upon us.
In the end, in the end –
other tides, other powers,
stay the heart, stay the flower.
Sto telos, sto telos –
I am home from the war,
I am home from the sea.

December 2015 North Andover, Mass

The Second Fiddle Speaks Out

The fiddle rests lightly,
cradled under my chin,
resting on my neck and skin.
I draw the bow
and the vibration in the bow
vibrates the string,
and the string, the wood of the fiddle,
and the wood, my neck.
We vibrate.
We're hummin' the same tune.

Before the concert,
the maestro looked at me.
I heard him speak,
but the words tripped
on their way through my ear.
What I heard was something
else, but
it was more wonderful
just the same.
So that's what I played.
Everyone looked on in amazement.

November 2015 Andover, Mass.

'Cuz I Love The Blues

I love the Blues.
When I hear that wail
coming from that place, so deep and sad,
so strong and frail –
When I hear that wail
carrying on through that despair of hope, somehow
climbing out of that hopeless, hopeless pit –
When I hear your voice
coming through as something else, something else,
coming through grievous and sorrowful, somehow
carrying a new heart, now grievous and true –
Why would I want you to feel that way?
Why would I want you to sing that song?
Why would I want you to walk that road?
'Cuz I love the Blues, I love the Blues.

But if that's wrong, if that's wrong –
then why would I take it away from you?
Why would I take it away?
It's the prize you earned,
your invisible scar,
a knife dragged through your soul,
making the scar that shines,
so beautiful in the night –
the night when you called out to God,
and all He had left to give you was your soul –
and somehow that let you take another step,
another step down the road,
somehow gave you strength,
gave you strength,
to carry on.

Why do I want you to feel that way?
Why do I want you to sing that song?
Why do I want you to walk that road?
'Cuz I walk that same road,
I walk that same road.
And that's why, that's why, that's why,
I love the Blues.

January 2016 North Andover, Mass.

A Bell Rings Thus

One bell rings from First Church.
The Revere bell rings out,
calling across common, town and wood.
One bell rings from First Church tower,
calling out, one bell, distant and plaintive,
rising and falling on the wind,
plain to me.
Counting time, counting forward, counting back,
one bell rings from First Church,
carrying time, carrying me, bearing me back.

Oh beautiful sound,
turning me from my desk,
turning me from my task,
rolling into my room above the ancient town,
calling across open air, into this open dormer,
you open a direct line from the cathedral tower.

From the cathedral tower, the bells are
calling falling ringing singing.
Calling above the old town, the bells are
bringing the morning, bringing their matins.
Ringing above gray streets, gray walls, gray folk,
reaching all, reaching me, the bells are
turning gray to gold.

Ringing ringing,
ye harmonies hidden in the air,
you are a standing ovation of angels
singing on assignment, a posting from heaven to us,
announcing your mysterious angelus.
Bestowing, naming or knowing?
Perhaps all, none or thus.

Ringing in tune, each bell is
turning spinning clapping laughing,
joining in harmony, together creating
this standing ovation of joy.
Assembling in the air above the town,
pouring into my ears, your sound is
standing angelic in the air.

My music teacher, you remind me
of heaven's harmonies in our world.
You are here all along,
but I forget, so I was sent
this ringing reminder.

Oh beautiful sound,
poured into the bells by the master bell maker then,
you are pouring your sound into my ears today.
Your first pouring is still ringing ringing.

The bell keeps ringing long after it was struck.
Now I am struck by your sound,
calling to me above the town,
ringing on your direct line.
In tune with yourself,
you are in tune with the world.
You do not need to be struck to ring.
You ring,
bringing gold to the gray town,
turning me from my task.
Ringing ringing,
oh beautiful sound,
a bell rings thus.

October 2015 North Andover, Mass.

A Door Opens

The bright day spills around the shades
drawn between the morning and the early afternoon.
In the darkened room,
the boy sits up on the bed,
naptime, tucked in, awake, waiting.
The door opens, a smiling face appears.
"See you later alligator."
The face disappears, the door closes, a laugh is shared.
The game at the door is played between mother and son.
"After a while crocodile."
Each open and close of the door
brings another laugh to share,
a smiling watch, an eager wait for more.
This is the playful game
of a mom and her five year old,
and how not to get a boy to take a nap.

There was love in your eyes
and you were looking at me.
I gazed back with the same playful joy,
knowing how much you cared about me
and how much I cared about you.
The door opens and closes.
Laughter and smiles are shared.
Playful joy and love fill the scene.

A look of joy across the room between mother and son
becomes a look across the years.
A gift you laid up for me now appears, fifty years on.
A gift you laid up for me is given today.
"See you later alligator."
There was love in your eyes
and you were looking at me
with your gift across the years.
"After a while crocodile."
When I was five and you were thirty-five,
with me at the start and you in the middle,
between the morning and the early afternoon,
with the bright day spilling around the shades,
a door opens between a mom and her boy.
So much love,
so much love yet to come.

Mother's Day 2016 North Andover, Mass.

Prayer Of The Rivers And The Land

Twin rivers of love and justice
flow from the source mountain.
They nourish the parched land.
They bring life
to where it had given up hope.
Waters of life they are,
surely as the water we drink.

Twin rivers of love and justice
travel over common ground.
They give shape
to the ground between us.
They make the land.
This land is a good place
to stand together,
in fair difference and shared purpose.

Twin rivers of love and justice
travel arm in arm, courses entwined.
They entwine in the valley
below the source mountain,
as they carry us to the pacific sea.

Twin rivers of love and justice –
May you bring life to our dry hearts.
May we be ready to receive your waters,
and not turn away from your courses.
May we be ready to drink deep
from your waters of life.
Twin rivers of love and justice
bring us strength and resolve,
carry us in your ease.
Amen.

January 2016 North Andover, Mass.

Abide

Rest
Wake
See
Feel
Think
Pray
Act
Love
Rest
Abide

A Crowd Of Joy At The Door

(2014 – 2015)

The Good Pilot – Introduction

My mom, Ann Marie (Behan) Bohrer, passed away on July 23, 2006, and my dad, Joe Bohrer Jr., passed on July 2, 2014. On the flight returning from my dad's funeral, with my son Nick sitting next to me on the plane, I sat there wanting to write a poem for my dad.

We were on the flight leg from Detroit to Seattle. I sat there on the plane and knew I had to write a poem for my dad.

I just started putting words down on paper. That's what they say – if you want to write something, start writing. The first two tries didn't go anywhere, but then the third try brought me the phrase "The Good Pilot", and the main idea and structure came with it whole, just like that. I never know how this happens, but somehow it does.

My dad was a private pilot. It was his passion. While we were growing up, Dad took us kids flying all the time. Thinking back to those flights, I can still visualize what Erie PA and the area around it looked like from the air. We heard about flying so much from him – it wasn't possible to have a conversation with him about any topic that didn't end up being redirected to be about flying! I was able to use some of the flying terms I heard all the time, and work them into the poem. For anyone who never met my dad, the "Good Pilot" means both pilot and man.

I wanted to read a poem at my father's funeral. I didn't have the right words that day. But that's what motivated me to write "The Good Pilot". As I wrote it returning from the funeral, it turned into something more - a love note to both my dad and my mom. I didn't know it would take that turn, but poems have a mind of their own.

Peace.

The Good Pilot

The good pilot knows his plane –
what it can do, what it can't.
Others might know takeoff power, rate of climb, service ceiling –
he knows how to restart an engine that's freezing.
He knows how to crab in a cross wind,
knows how to land it dead stick.

The good pilot knows his way 'round the sky –
when to fly under clouds, when to turn back.
Others might know albedo, isotherm or wind shear –
the clouds he can read, he knows weather by feel.
He knows how to navigate storms when they darken,
knows how to fly those dark valleys of heaven.

The good pilot knows his route
to the home field today.
No need for a chart, no flight plan is filed,
he vectors on final, he pilots by heart.
The instruction is done, no more touch and go's,
all his flight hours logged, at last returns to his love.

At the home field she waits, sees the wheels kiss the ground –
takes in his last taxi and turn, her vigil ends at the gate.
Patient during the post flight, magnetos check, engine off –
she knows her man, was willing to wait.
She opens the door as he flies through,
again they are one, no longer two.
The good pilot is home.

July 2014 Written in the air, somewhere over America
In memory of my Dad, Joe Bohrer, Jr., the good pilot, and my Mom, Ann Marie, his love

Bradstreet School Still Stands – Introduction
January 2015

This poem had its start in December 2014 when I drove past the then shuttered Bradstreet School. Somehow that day the sight of the old school building sitting by itself behind the closed gate, surrounded by the snowy schoolyard, gave me an idea for a poem. My daughter had gone to kindergarten at Bradstreet when it was last in use as an Early Childhood Education Center. I felt sad to see it sit there empty and unused for so long, and I felt this even more keenly when the town decided that it should be torn down.

For a few weeks I mulled over these thoughts. Then I parked there one Saturday afternoon in December and put the thoughts on paper. The poem is what resulted.

I've enjoyed reading poetry all my life, but only recently read Anne Bradstreet's poems. I was really amazed at how good and accessible they are, even after these centuries. She was really a remarkable woman. And this town was her home. I tried to capture something of the spirit she conveyed, and my feelings about Bradstreet School.

I've since heard that Bradstreet School was actually named after Anne's husband, Simon Bradstreet, who was governor of the Massachusetts Bay Colony. But where Simon spent much of his life away in Boston in service to the colony, Anne lived and wrote here in this town, and I feel that the name of Bradstreet School is hers as much as Simon's.

I've written poetry before, but was especially happy to write a poem about and for North Andover. I hope people think about all of those who dedicated their lives to teaching the children of our town over the years - and centuries.

If you'd like to read some of you Anne Bradstreet's poems, you can find them here: http://annebradstreet.org/annes-poems/
The site is the work of "The Friends of Anne Bradstreet",
chaired by Karen M. Kline, former Poet Laureate of North Andover.

January 2015
North Andover, Mass.

Introduction - Addendum
March 2018

On March 15, 2018, the School Committee voted unanimously to name the town's new school the "Anne Bradstreet Early Childhood Center". As a result, North Andover finally has a school named in her honor.

Bradstreet School Still Stands

The old brick façade gazes silently down,
watching the quiet yard of school days past.
Empty halls echo, life and lessons are done.
Windows stand dark, the welcome door is held fast.
For these brick walls, the bell has rung.

Here lively feet and playful voices once gathered.
Days began with a class on the swings and bars.
So keen to learn – a jest – not all so eager
for the school mistress bell to sound the start.
Take your seat, hands folded, sit straight for teacher.
Pens out, books open, the lesson's begun.

Perhaps the hand of an earlier mistress
guided their pens, though her hand held a quill.
She walked the same land, a poet's page was her canvas.
She reared her own, with goodly words instill'd.
In the verse that she wrote – to her child not yet born –
was it meant for those who gathered here each morn?

Perhaps you saw far to your red brick namesake.
Would you nod your assent, to what your words began,
to lessons learned under your good gentle name?
Surely taught – as by your own careful hand –
the pupils and teachers you trained,
your descendants became.

The purpose that guided the build of this frame
has carried on to other rooms, other doors.
This mistress is left, behind her fence, her gate.
Decision made, by town citizens okayed,
this red brick lady will stand no more.

Only some stores, in-town homes, and a plaque.
Leaving the mind's eye, and a gift, in the heart
of those with town colors of scarlet and black,
of those in her care who studied and taught,
of those with the spirit of sturdy red brick.

The good gentle spirit of our mistress poet,
with her own at her knee as she taught and pen'd,
has carried on to those who were not yet born,
has carried on to those who guide with sure hand,
has carried on to those who teach all as their own.

When this brick lady is gone,
some will yet understand –
Bradstreet school is still here.
Bradstreet school still stands.

December 2014 North Andover, Mass.

Knowing

Whatever happens, this I know –
I am loved.
Whether I am right or wrong,
whether I speak with the voice of love
or of mud,
I am still loved.
I try to do right,
but when I fail,
miss the mark,
slip off the track,
this I know –
I am still loved.
It takes honest effort to repair,
and the effort is worth something I know,
but whether I am right or wrong
you give me
the simplest gift
that starts with knowing
I am loved
by you.

March 2014 North Andover, Mass.

Play On

Am I willing to be open today
Naked to the world
Standing here as I am
Where – that's all I have – is enough
Am I willing

Am I willing to be hurt again
Yet another day
Am I willing to be naked on this stage
Oh those slings and arrows
Of easy and quick misunderstanding
And so much worse
That we all throw at one another
Built into our existence
Our outrageous fortune
Not our true intent with one another
But there
But there

Am I willing to not be the same
To get past the simple game
To act with love, to play the higher game
But either way
I'm in the play

Am I willing to offer a flower in my hand
But, hah, I'm a man
A warrior, now with a flower in his hand!

Wait, see what's here
The bud of this flower is in every moment
Inside is the message of this hour
I want to open it

Am I willing to be open today
Am I willing to stand on this stage
Am I willing to stand here as I am
To still be strong
And to play on

June 2014 North Andover, Mass.

Across The Knife Edge

Following the cold trail across the high country,
somewhere in front of us the other summit rises,
invisible in the icy windswept fog.
We must reach the safety of the other side
before the coming storm
reaches us.

Across the knife edge,
faster and faster we go
into the fog of the day.
Along the tumbled edge,
giant rocks make us twist and turn.
Some are hewn too large for us to step.
Faster and faster we go,
into the fog of the day,
into the invisible future.

Across the knife edge,
the path narrows as we climb,
but we don't see it yet.
Why don't we see it?
Hunting, hunting
for ground beneath our feet.
Will we stop or turn
before it falls away –
Why don't we see it?
Hunting, hunting
for ground beneath our feet.

Across the knife edge,
into the fog of the day,
through the wind, ahead of the storm,
to the safety of the other side,
into the invisible future,
we race.

May 2014 North Andover, Mass.

94

Ozymandias In Reverse

Long ago, we stood in this antique land.
Back when the land was young,
we gazed upon the stones, so many to see.
We tread upon their form,
so many about this land, so many under our feet.
We looked as far as we could see,
to the horizon, then not so far,
back when time was young.
Did we wonder at what would be?

These are the stones that remain.
These are not the stones
selected by the builder.
These are the stones
that time could not take away.
Tell me what's of value,
and now we all say these stones, yes these.
Don't you see?
These stones make the great tower that's here.
And today we all say,
look how far we can see from these heights!

But we can't see far enough
to know how this tower came to be.
We can't see far enough
to know how these stones came to be.
The stones and tower we see
were here all along.
Everything else that couldn't stand
the tests and trials of time
was taken away.
These are the greater.
The lesser is gone.

These are the stones that remain.
Where they are
is not where they were placed.
This is the tower that remains.
Where it stands
is not where it was built.
How can this be?

The hand of another builder
made these, made this.
The eye of another builder
placed these, placed this.
With awful might
this work was raised for us.
Do we know what we've been given?

Long ago we walked along these ramparts,
reached them with an easy step.
Only time made their height known to us.
What else don't we know?

August 2014 North Andover, Mass

On The Old Wooden Roller-Coaster

That smell of old wood, old steel, old machine oil –
that same smell every summer –
makes us wonder –
how old is that wood?
But into the roller-coaster cars –
angling past one another –
willingly we climb.

The attendant walks death row
like a bailiff, closing the bars
two by two, locks us in.
That sound – click, click, clank –
makes us wonder –
how good is that latch?
But in the last car we sit –
experts of the experience –
impatiently we wait.

Throwing the long arm, he finally releases the brake.
To the bottom of the big hill, we roll and shake.
Onto the gear chain, with a clink and a yank,
we feel the machine, as we're pulled to our fate.

The view of nothing
suddenly appears over the top –
makes us wonder –
why are we doing this, and how can we stop?
But the machine is in charge –
our hands can only tighten the bar –
eagerly we grip.

Waiting, waiting, for gravity to take hold –
oh, for that old delicious drop –
when that invisible hand pulls the cars
and then us
over the top.
We have one last thought –
this is what we wanted.

November 2014 North Andover, Mass.

From The Christening

Those who came before us
are not gone,
even though they rest today
in quiet fields of stone and flower.

Those we love who are gone
live in mind and heart,
their home,
alive in love's power.

But more than this,
those who came before
and gave us life,
or read stories to us at a Sunday visit,
played games together at the family picnic,
gazed out the window with us during the storm —
arms around —
or held us at the christening,
still live I claim.

Look back through the lens of time.
Follow the unseen line of sight,
not my invention,
but one that science calls dimension.

This story tells of an unbroken line, a celestial strand,
a woven thread of strength eternal.
The eternal now.

Now.
The ones we love
are still as they were,
alive and strong,
though passed from our easy view.
They still move and breathe,
laugh and sing,
on that line of time,
as real as yesterday,
like friends who moved away
now living in another town.
But we're the ones who moved.
Still, that strand is in our reach.

I feel the threads return and join,
connecting to the fabric here
that I now hold in hand,
this fabric of the gown passed down
from the christening.

For Aunt Mary Jo
April 2014 North Andover, Mass.

Waiting In The Colonial Churchyard

Waiting in the churchyard
For something to save me
Waiting in the churchyard
Stillness comes to me

Here is the quiet steady God of Franklin and Jefferson
Persistent as the field grass
Good unbidden, though not undeserved
Mine to have, yours as well
God in the world
To be gathered like wild wheat
Nature's honey or free grown grapes
Like the colonist's self-reliance
I am better saved if I save myself
But isn't that gift of salvation
Still freely provided, wildly sown for me?
To be saved from myself, by myself
God still rightly gets the kudos
God in the world
God of the world
God for the world
God in us
God of us
God for us
Stillness in the churchyard is what I see
Quiet goodness is what I feel
I am glad

June 2014   North Andover, Mass.

Church Hour

This one hour
This view from the center
A feeling of movement all around
But here, this calm center
Around which everything pivots
The center holds
The center of this wheel
The center of this week
I feel it now
Centripetal force now
Not the common opposite
Here things don't fly apart
They come together
Like the sun with his careful hold
On those wanderers in the far sky
He holds, she holds, they hold,
The spirit holds
This calming center
Such jovial gravity
Fills and holds this quiet center
All at once
Joyous, brimming, bursting, buzzing
Glowing, swelling, soaring, singing
Joyous
Together

June 2014 North Andover, Mass.

Surprised

God is surprised
by what takes place.
Aren't you?
The next turn of events,
God knows not.
He wants to find out.
Don't you?
Otherwise, She might say,
what would be the point?
If there was no choice about it,
God would not want that world –
if it were all pre-ordained, pre-cast.
So instead –
God is surprised.

It's so much more fun
to know not
how the dice will finish their roll.
Will good come out on top?
Or will it need another try?
God wants to find out.
Don't you?

That's the reason
All was started.
God wanted to find out
what this world might be –
if given the chance.
What we might be –
if given the choice.

Isn't it surprising that God –
All Knowing, All Powerful,
All Omniscient, All Omnipotent –
Yah, yah, we've heard all of that, all of that –
so isn't it surprising
that what happens next,
God knows not.
Think about it –
when we say that God
has infinite knowledge and power –
it's like saying that the ocean
is infinitely wet
just because it holds all the water.
Surprise.

God is still surprised.
Even with all of this all-ness,
God needs to let it play out –
wants to see what happens.
And hopes someday
to be pleasantly surprised
when good comes out on top.

September 2014 North Andover, Mass.

The Source Valley

I came upon the source valley
at night, under stars and a late full moon.
Named by homesteaders, perhaps wrongly,
for a source spring miles to the west,
for that was how they first came upon the valley.
From that, the valley had a local name.

Another restless night, I set out to hike,
the brown lab willing to join my moonlight foray.
Blackie stayed in bed.
Starting on our familiar trail, I felt safe.
From the camp house, through the pine stand, to the shore,
we headed out.
Because the moon was bright,
I took the new path, cleared by the crew last fall.

I came upon the source valley
at night, when echoes from the cliffs reached me.
Stopping and standing, where the ground dropped away –
sounds of rushing waters, far below –
powerful water, cascading over rocks and falls, far below –
here in the dark, under trees, along the cliff,
I grew uncertain of the path.

Echoes from the source valley
reached me where the trail stopped.
The moon took a chance and dropped behind a cloud,
leaving me in the starlight –
the dog strangely quiet, at my feet –
the dark valley unseen.

The deep tones of water and the night,
both searching for their course,
are sounding, echoing through me.
Standing still,
my night walk took a different course.

Soundings of deep blue
echo in the unseen valley.
I looked down, as if down is strength,
as if I could find strength in sadness and loss,
as if I needed the dark
to see in front of me.

Soundings from the source valley,
the deep tones I cannot name,
reach me in the night.
Standing on the ridge, above the source valley,
the water courses through me.
I am quenched.

August 2014 North Andover, Mass.

A Pocket To Carry On The Journey

She touches my hand. I am awake.
Her face already tells me
what she came in to say.
We have word. They're coming.
Your chance for a break.
There is little time. You must be away.

Into my hand, she presses bread.
Eat now, and here, take this.
You'll need it, for the road ahead.
The cheese is hard, but the fruit is good.
Take this for strength today.
And here, take this coat, for warmth tonight.
You'll need this. Take it. She stops, faces me.
I know you'll be strong, but take this too.
She presses my hands, hers on mine.
Carry the curve of my hands with yours.
When you open and close yours,
the curve of my hands will be with you.
Whatever strength I have, here it is. Take it.

Into my hand, she places
an old leather pouch, a pocket.
I turn, quizzical. She speaks.
Inside is my letter, a note.
Read it tomorrow. I'll be with you then.
She pauses, a sideways look and a smile.
Inside you'll find more, carefully hidden.
I look inside. Except for the note,
there's nothing to see.

Gathering my hands, she looks straight at me.
Inside it are things, hidden away –
things that once given, no one can take –
stories shared, songs we sing, common dreams.
They can't be taken, but you can share.
Carry this with you. Bring it out when you need.
She smiles.
You have this
most of all
when there's nothing to see.
Into my hand, she places the pocket.
A pocket to carry on the journey.
Take it.

December 2014 North Andover, Mass.

What You Have

Don't forget what you have
Everything, that's all
It's all yours
No one can take it away
The universe and everything in it are yours
What did you think
It was someone else's?
How could that be?
It was given to you at your birth
A gift of the gods
As you were their gift
To the world
Don't smile, it's true
I've seen it
With my eyes
And my heart
Neither gift can be taken away
Be true to these gifts
Especially where they meet
In your heart
Don't forget what you have
Don't forget
Oh and one more gift
You were also given today

October 2014 North Andover, Mass.

A Crowd Of Joy At The Door

(Directions: read as fast as you can)

Yes I feel this good this good this good
Words are spilling out in a torrent of
Joy joy joy bursting through the door
Overflowing with happy and sad, mean and fine, low and high
And aching aching aching
But joy joy joy bursting through the door
A tripping rush of joy, spilling splashing splashing
Pouring into this new world, painting a new new day
A crowd of joy at the door

Yes I feel this fine this fine this fine
You've got to listen listen listen to this
You've got to hear this and this and this
Words crowd to get out, get out of the way
Joy joy joy bursting through the door
Splashes of color, splashes of flavor in the old gray
Painting our minds with kaleidoscope eyes
Out of their minds and into our skies
No longer for you blue
A crowd of joy at the door
A strawberry field in bloom in an instant
Please please pleasing
So wanting to be heard
A crowd of joy at the door
Yes love

August 2014 North Andover, Mass.
PS. Yes, this is about the Beatles and a love of their music...

Into The Mystic Pint

Ah, The Guinness.
Another fine draw of the mystic pint.
Whether 'tis nobler when poured in the glass,
or when poured down the throat,
'tis a question to ponder indeed,
said one barrister to the other.
But 'tis not such a conundrum
so worthy of debate at the bar
as long as there be
another bottle on the wall, of said bar.
Or even better,
said the other barrister,
another keg in the cellar, of said bar.
And at said bar, what a fine judge you are!
Truly noble indeed!
Yes, thank you, dear friend,
I would take another draw.
'Twould be a mistake to ponder further.

Ah, The Guinness!
Another fine draw of the mystic pint!
Magnificently we will flow
into the mystic indeed.

January 2015 North Andover, Mass.

Small Universe

(1979 – 1987)

The future offers freedom, the one rare gift of time.

A Fallen Day

Tramping through leaves on winters edge
A cold lark sings above my head
A like wind through blew clear and strong
A higher voice, a hidden song
Heard once on a fallen day
Enjoying leaves that wouldn't stay
Running along
I play

Tramping through leaves I sing my song
Though not so cold and clear and strong
But taking in the sounds there heard
Of wind and leaves and high sung bird
Heard once on a fallen day
Enjoying leaves that wouldn't stay
Singing along
I play

1979 Florissant, Missouri

For A Friend In Unknown Difficulty

When a flower in the desert blooms
Unbeknownst to God
Or any lesser force that might stop it
It has to be good
To give itself unknown to help me
Help me face the truth
Good comes unasked
Even when all that is
Stands undeserving
To be
It has to be greater
Than any ordered stay
It is it is just ask me
I've seen the flower bloom
To challenge a desert day

1986 West Newton, Mass

Nothing Said

Damn
She found my mantra
What do I do?

She said it as she was saying hello
Like a sister, friend
Just in passing
How are you, oh? Umm?
Ah there
Open your hand, take mine up
Make me jump
Already yours, do you know why?

Did you say what?
Or was it just a slip? A trip?
Did you know?
Doesn't matter, the universe knows
When a tree falls
Or a man, wakes to
Nothing said, so much known
About you, can I
Tell you about me?

1986 West Newton, Mass.

Heights

The end of the road
Has a silence watched
Like bud gone past full flower
Or a hillside filled with leaves

The end of the road
Has power
Of unmet, broken dreams

Without loves whispered answers
Only quiet draw
Of paces walked in stillness
And heights seen from afar

New Worlds

Oh to be flung by the hand of life
Spun into dreams unseen, so ready for sight
Hurled out of the palm, flat on a flight
True on a course, across star-filled night
Bound for who knows where

But the direction is known
The direction is known
Think

The sense comes from all around you
The force that spins suns through space
Brings order and good and new worlds to the light
This hand guides you where you fly
Trust it

1985 West Newton, Mass.

118

U2

I expect nothing
give nothing
show nothing
I expect all
give all
show all
Die in pain and
in laughter
Cut me to bits
and feed me
to your friends
If I did the same
to you
Would you laugh
I would
U2?

In Your Cause

The radio has been following me around
For days it speaks
With words I don't even have
A chance to form
There it is concluding my thoughts
Or opening a phrase
That I rush to finish
It's all about you
And damn the radio
For acting on its own
Speaking out from the larger world
With all its vain attempts
To get me back to you

1986 West Newton, Mass.

This Night

(i)

I heard my mother's voice
Calling through the silence of the night
With warning to awaken
Was there something I might forget?
Oh no, just the notice
That my package had arrived
From West Suburban Cleveland
A box of books and papers
Of heroes of the past
Ohio sends these gentle minders
When we get astray
When we long for that voice not ending
A nap on a dark hot summer day
When we long for that voice not ending
This night
Now many miles away

(ii)

Did you kiss me tonight
Brush my cheek as I lay sleeping
To let me know
All was right
With us and the world
Passing your gift
Of acceptance and love
To one who needs it
And awakens thinking of you
This night
Now many miles away

1986 West Newton, Mass.

The Physician

Out in the middle of nowhere
Where everything is happening
Where particles scream for existence
Straining at the bonds that hold them
From boiling into being

This is the physic
Where all that is not
Constantly seeks to be
In the spaces of what is
And finally, to push aside
That which gave it space
With what wants to be

1986 West Newton, Mass.

Holes Again

When the fabric of sense
Won't stretch to fit
And the damn holes show through
Of God knows what
I do worry
What if I get used to this

The Advocate

When love speaks
It pushes aside harder thoughts
With a soft insistent voice

It tells me to listen through the din
To what I'm missing
The quiet cause
That has no lobby
Petitioning for action in its name
Sometimes without ally

Years go by unheard
It still speaks to me when I go wrong
It teaches me again and again
This forever unfinished lesson
How to be kind

1986 West Newton, Mass.

SIDE VIEW

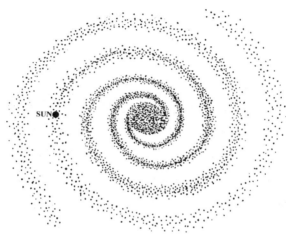

SUN

TOP VIEW

<u>a poem is</u>
a suitcase of words
packed with brain, heart, and soul
ready for travel

A SHORT BIO

∞ ∞ ∞ ∞ ∞ ∞ ∞ ∞ ∞ ∞ ∞ ∞ ∞

Mark Bohrer
has designed software to track satellites,
written and given sermons,
run marathons,
managed people and projects,
served as a church deacon,
stood atop the roof of Notre Dame Cathedral
(sadly now, before the fire),
held a pint of ale in a Salisbury pub,
gazed up at the open skylight in the Pantheon in Rome,
and volunteered on the Bradstreet School PTO.
He is a husband and a dad.

Born and raised in Erie, Pennsylvania,
he moved to New England in 1982.
He's lived in North Andover, Massachusetts since 1997.

He currently serves as the Poet Laureate of the town.

∞ ∞ ∞ ∞ ∞ ∞ ∞ ∞ ∞ ∞ ∞ ∞ ∞